20 FUN FACTS ABOUT WOMEN IN ANCIENT GREECE AND ROME

By Kristen Rajczak

Gareth Stevens
PUBLISHING

Please visit our website, www.garethstevens.com. For a free color catalog of all our high-quality books, call toll free 1-800-542-2595 or fax 1-877-542-2596.

Library of Congress Cataloging-in-Publication Data

Rajczak, Kristen.
  20 fun facts about women in ancient Greece and Rome / Kristen Rajczak.
     pages cm. — (Fun fact file: Women in history)
  Includes bibliographical references and index.
  ISBN 978-1-4824-2816-2 (pbk.)
  ISBN 978-1-4824-2817-9 (6 pack)
  ISBN 978-1-4824-2818-6 (library binding)
  1. Women—Greece—History—To 1500—Juvenile literature. 2. Women—Rome—History—Juvenile literature.
3. Women—History—To 500—Juvenile literature. 4. Sex role—Greece—History—To 1500—Juvenile literature. 5.
Sex role—Rome—History—Juvenile literature. 6. Greece—Social conditions—To 146 B.C.—Juvenile literature. 7.
Rome—Social conditions—Juvenile literature. I. Title. II. Title: Twenty fun facts about women in ancient Greece
and Rome.
  HQ1134.R34 2016
  305.40938—dc23

                                    2015006053

First Edition

Published in 2016 by
Gareth Stevens Publishing
111 East 14th Street, Suite 349
New York, NY 10003

Copyright © 2016 Gareth Stevens Publishing

Designer: Samantha DeMartin
Editor: Kristen Rajczak

Photo credits: Cover, p 1 Bridgeman Art Library/The Bridgeman Art Library/Getty Images; p. 5 Daderot/
Wikimedia Commons; p. 6 DEA PICTURE LIBRARY/De Agostini/Getty Images; p. 7 Dirsmith1/Wikimedia
Commons; pp. 8, 13 Wonderlane/Wikimedia Commons; p. 9 DEA/G. DAGLI ORTI/De Agostini/Getty Images;
p. 10 Class of Hamburg 1917.477/Wikimedia Commons; pp. 11, 25, 29 DEA/G. DAGLI ORTI/De Agostini
Picture Library/Getty Images; p. 12 DEA/G. NIMATALLAH/De Agostini/Getty Images; p. 14 Bibi Saint-Pol/
Wikimedia Commons; pp. 15, 16, 22 Print Collector/Hulton Archive/Getty Images; p. 17 Hein Nouwens/
Shutterstock.com; pp. 18, 20 Hulton Archive/Hulton Archive/Getty Images; p. 19 Cbailel9/Wikimedia
Commons; p. 21 PHAS/Universal Images Group/Getty Images; p. 23 Pasicles/Wikimedia Commons;
p. 24 Wellcome Images/Wikimedia Commons; p. 26 Milos Bicanski/Getty Images Sport/Getty Images.

CPSIA compliance information: Batch #CS15GS: For further information contact Gareth Stevens, New York, New York at 1-800-542-2595.

Contents

Words in the glossary appear in **bold** type the first time they are used in the text.

Looking to History

A Greek historian from the fifth century BC wrote, "The greatest glory [for women] is to be least talked about among men, whether in praise or blame." In ancient Greece and Rome, it was men's opinion of women that mattered most.

Today, historians are taking a closer look at women's place, or role, in these societies—and they've found out a lot! Women's lives were just as interesting as men's, though their roles were often less public. Some women even did things to change history!

Men wrote much of what's known about women in ancient Greece and Rome. They wrote that a woman should obey her father or husband and be happy to keep his house. This wasn't always true!

FACT 1

The Greek city of Athens is called the first democracy, but women couldn't vote!

Though it was believed that all male citizens should have a say in government, women had almost no rights in ancient Athens. Their place was in the home, caring for children, preparing meals, and making clothing.

Greek men spent a lot of time away from home. That left women a lot to do! However, most women had slaves to help them.

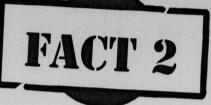

A Roman woman's number one job was to raise children to be model Roman citizens.

In most cases, a woman's major duty was running her husband's household. That included teaching the children how to be good Romans who followed the laws and worked hard in the **empire**.

Though Roman women had few rights, mothers were valued for their part in giving birth to and raising the future citizens of Rome.

7

FACT 3

In ancient Greece, women lived to about age 40 on average.

Women had three major stages of life. A young woman was called a *kore*. When she married, she became a *nymphe*, or bride. Finally, when she became a mother, she was a *gyne*, or woman.

Roman women sealed their marriage with a kiss.

In ancient Rome, love wasn't often part of marriage like it is today. However, Roman brides did wear white! They also had bridesmaids, and weddings were followed by a big party.

In both ancient Greece and Rome, fathers chose husbands for their daughters.

FACT 5

Greek women didn't often meet men outside of their family until they got married.

Women didn't spend much time outside of their home. Young women were expected to almost totally cover their face and head when they went out. They were only supposed to talk with close female neighbors and family.

Motherhood and Beyond

Women who had three babies were given independence in Rome.

About 25 percent of babies died in the first year of their life during the first century AD. Babies who lived were highly prized—so much so that the Roman government rewarded successful mothers.

FACT 7

Spartan mothers did **physical** training to prepare for motherhood.

The Greek **city-state** of Sparta recognized that mothers were the first to **influence** children. They needed to perform physical feats much like those their sons would someday in order to raise the best soldiers they could.

Girls from the city-state of Athens had some schooling in preparation for their household role.

Once a wealthy woman's husband died, she became a widow—and an independent woman.

Roman women were under their father's control until they married. Then their husband was in charge. In the upper classes, husbands were commonly older than their wife. Women were often teenagers when they married.

Women married to men with some power, such as in the government, often had some influence on them and their work.

FACT 9

To dye their hair black, Roman women covered their hair with leeches mixed with vinegar and sat in the sun to bake the mix into their hair.

Other popular colors women—and men—dyed their hair included blonde and a red-gold color. Women also curled their hair and pinned it up in fancy styles.

Greek women wore colorful, decorative clothing.

Greek men and women had similar clothing, often made of cloth like wool or linen. They wore long pieces of cloth pinned at the shoulder and often tied at the waist. Both men and women might wear soft shoes or sandals, but commonly went barefoot at home.

Historians have learned about what women wore by looking at ancient Greek art, such as vases.

Wealthy Roman women had a special servant called a *vestiplica* who helped ready their clothing.

Most Roman clothing was wool, but later cotton, silk, and

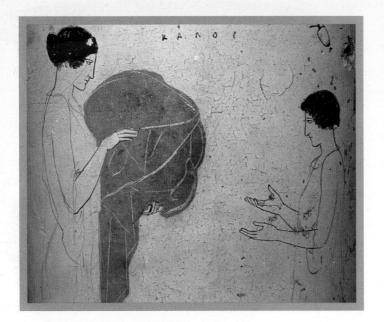

other kinds of cloth could be bought by those with enough money. Clothing was folded or hung on the body based on the day's fashions.

Later in the Roman Empire, cloth was brought in from all over the world for the fashions of the wealthy.

Clothing of a Roman Woman

head scarf

palla (worn over the stola, made of wool)

stola (tunic, or long, loose piece of clothing)

Roman women were very interested in fashion! Their clothing was often brightly colored, especially if the woman was wealthy.

FACT 12

Some Roman women chose to train and fight as gladiators.

Like men, women could be forced to fight for sport.

However, even those who wanted to be gladiators were less

respected and less popular than male gladiators.

Gladiators were trained fighters. They often fought to the death.

A Spartan woman won two Olympic chariot races in 396 BC and 392 BC.

Cynisca was the sister of a Spartan king. She trained horses and chose men to race them in the Olympics. Though her teams won the chariot race twice, it's unlikely she was even allowed to watch them!

At the time Cynisca won her chariot races, the Olympics had already been happening for about 400 years!

19

FACT 14

A group of Greek female poets were named the "nine earthly muses."

Much of the writing women poets did in ancient Greece hasn't survived to present day. Anyte of Tegea wrote most of the work that still exists. She was one of the first poets to write about the natural world around her rather than the gods.

Greek women played major roles in religious festivals.

Festivals were special occasions and some of the only times that women might work with men. There were also women-only festivals. These often had to do with praying for a good harvest. Additionally, young girls might serve in certain goddesses' temples.

The ancient Greeks celebrated many festivals. Many of them were to honor the gods.

FACT 16

A Roman woman owned a large farming business with farms in Africa, Spain, and beyond during the fifth century AD.

Not all women stayed at home! Another woman, Eumachia, made so much money in her brick business, she paid for public buildings in the city of Pompeii.

A **volcano** destroyed Pompeii in AD 79. The volcanic rock preserved, or saved, what was happening that day in stone. Many who have studied the remains have found clues to the daily lives of Romans, including women.

A woman named Hypatia invented the astrolabe.

Hypatia was a mathematician and **astronomer** who lived and worked in the city of Alexandria when it was part of the Roman Empire. During her time, the later years of the Roman Empire, girls had started going to school more.

Hypatia

FACT 18

Roman emperor Augustus's wife had political rivals killed so her son could become emperor.

Livia Drusilla had two children with her first husband before marrying Caesar Augustus. When Augustus died, she made sure her son Tiberius, though not Augustus's son, would become emperor—at any cost.

Livia Drusilla often served as an adviser to the emperor. When he was away from Rome, they wrote letters to each other on many topics.

Olympias might have been the greatest influence—man or woman—on Greece in the fourth century BC.

Mother of Alexander the Great, Olympias may have killed her husband and others to make sure Alexander became the next ruler. She advised Alexander and protected his son until her own imprisonment and death.

Olympias

FACT 20

Goddesses were believed to have great power, just as gods were.

Both men and women honored goddesses, such as Hera, Athena, and Demeter. In fact, Athena was the goddess of Athens, and her temple still stands atop the famous Athenian Acropolis, which overlooks the city.

The Parthenon was Athena's temple on the Acropolis.

Goddesses

goddess of...	Greek name	Roman name
love	Aphrodite	Venus
the moon and the hunt	Artemis	Diana
wisdom and war for just causes	Athena	Minerva
the harvest	Demeter	Ceres
marriage and queen of the gods	Hera	Juno
the hearth and home	Hestia	Vesta

Goddesses were an important part of Greek and Roman **mythology**. Romans worshiped Greek goddesses under different names. Use this chart to find out about some of the major goddesses, including both their Greek and Roman names.

Always More to Learn

It's clear that ancient Greek and Roman men valued women for their role as mothers. They weren't given any real say in governing, yet it was mothers who often influenced the most powerful men! Women were able to show their worth, even if it's only in history that we can see it.

There's more to be discovered about the lives of women in ancient Greece and Rome. In time, we may know many more fun facts!

The goddesses of Greek and Roman mythology have been part of art for centuries! This image is from the 19th century.

Glossary

astrolabe: a scientific tool used to see the positions of moons, stars, and planets

astronomer: a person who studies stars, planets, and other heavenly bodies

city-state: a government in which an independent city rules over the surrounding area as well as itself

democracy: a form of government in which all citizens take part

empire: a large area of land under the control of a single ruler

influence: to have an effect on

muse: someone who provides another with inspiration. There are nine sister goddesses in Greek mythology called the Muses.

mythology: all the myths, or stories, that deal with a culture's gods and heroes

physical: having to do with the body

religious: having to do with a belief in and way of honoring a god or gods

rival: one of two or more working to have something only one can have

volcano: an opening in a planet's surface through which hot, liquid rock sometimes flows

For More Information

Books

England, Victoria. *Top 10 Worst Things About Ancient Greece: You Wouldn't Want to Know.* New York, NY: Sandy Creek, 2013.

Ridley, Sarah. *Life in Ancient Greece.* Mankato, MN: Smart Apple Media, 2015.

Wolfson, Evelyn. *Mythology of the Romans.* Berkeley Heights, NJ: Enslow Publishers, Inc., 2014.

Websites

Ancient Greeks
www.bbc.co.uk/schools/primaryhistory/ancient_greeks/
Learn more about what life was like in ancient Greece here.

Ten Facts About Ancient Rome
www.ngkids.co.uk/did-you-know/10-facts-about-the-ancient-Romans
Do you want to know more about ancient Rome? Find cool facts on this website!

Index